FASCINATING SCIENCE PROJECTS

ELECTRICITY and MAGNETISM

Bobbi Searle

Franklin Watts
London • Sydney

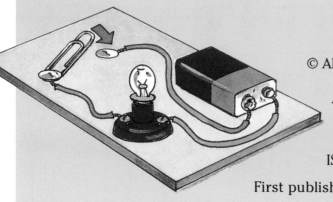

© Aladdin Books Ltd 2002
Produced by
Aladdin Books Ltd
28 Percy Street
London W1T 2BZ

ISBN 0–7496–4478–8

First published in Great Britain in 2002 by
Franklin Watts
96 Leonard Street
London
EC2A 4XD

Designers:
Flick, Book Design and Graphics
Ian Thompson

Editor:
Harriet Brown

Illustrators:
Andrew Geeson, Catherine Ward
and Peter Wilks – SGA
Cartoons:
Tony Kenyon – BL Kearley

Consultant:
Bryson Gore

Printed in Belgium

A CIP catalogue record for this book is available
from the British Library.

Contents

What is electricity? 6
Make a fan powered by
electricity and see how switches
turn electricity on and off

Current 10
Discover how current can
make a motor spin

Batteries 14
See how a chemical reaction
can create electricity

Static electricity 18
Make your own lightning

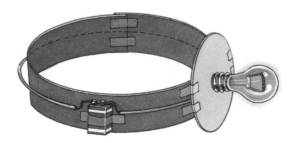

All around you 22
Make a secret room alarm
and discover how a balloon
can light a bulb

What is magnetism? 26
Make your own magnetic boat
and make a song disappear

Magnetic poles 30
Make a water compass and
find out how magnets can hover

Magnetic fields 34
Discover what magnetic fields look
like and make a magnetic shield

Electromagnetism 38
Make an electromagnetic crane and
see how electricity magnetises metal

Amazing magnets 42
Make a coin sorter and find
iron in your breakfast cereal

Glossary 46

Index 48

Introduction

In this book, the science of electricity and magnetism is explained through a series of fascinating projects and experiments. Each chapter deals with a different topic on electricity and magnetism and contains a major project that is supported by simple experiments, 'Magic panels' and 'Fascinating fact' boxes. At the end of every chapter is an explanation of what has happened and what this means. Projects requiring sharp tools should be done under adult supervision.

This states the purpose of the project

METHOD NOTES
Helpful hints on things to remember when carrying out your project.

Materials
In this box is a full list of the items needed to carry out each main project.

1. The steps that describe how to carry out each project are listed clearly as numbered points.

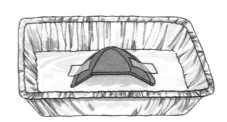

Figure 2

2. Where there are illustrations to help you understand the instructions, the text refers to them as Figure 1, etc.

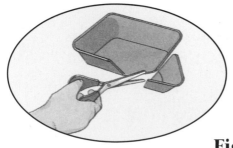

Figure 1

THE AMAZING MAGIC PANEL
This heading states what is happening

These boxes contain an activity or experiment that has a particularly dramatic or surprising result!

WHY IT WORKS
You can find out exactly what happened here too.

WHY IT WORKS

These boxes, headed 'Why it works', contain an explanation of what happened during your project, and the meaning of the result.

Fascinating facts!
An amusing or surprising fact related to the theme of the chapter.

Never use electricity with wet hands. Make sure an adult knows what you are doing. If a project involves using a sharp knife, you will see this symbol. Always use insulated wire.

The text in these circles links the theme of the topic from one page to the next in the chapter.

What is electricity?

Electricity is a form of energy on which our daily lives depend. Many things in our homes and schools are powered by electricity. It provides energy in the form of heat to make light bulbs glow, and electrical impulses to make our computers work. Without it our transport systems would not work and we wouldn't be able to communicate using telephones, emails or text messages.

See how electricity can power a fan

METHOD NOTES
Hold your fan away from your face and eyes when you are using it.

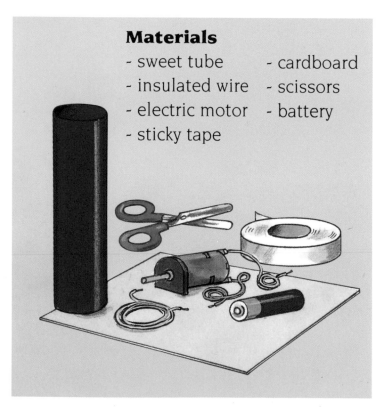

Materials

- sweet tube	- cardboard
- insulated wire	- scissors
- electric motor	- battery
- sticky tape	

1. Take the lid off a sweet tube and push the bottom out of the other end.
2. Cut two pieces of wire so that they are as long as the tube. Twist one end of each wire tightly onto each terminal at the back end of the motor (Figure 1).

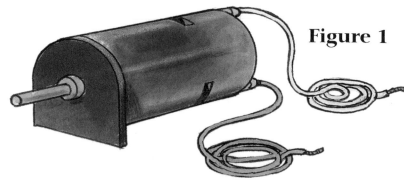

Figure 1

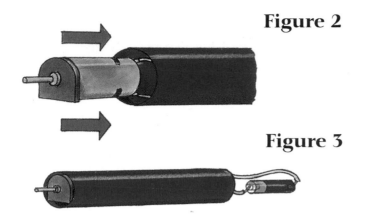

Figure 2

Figure 3

3. Push the motor backwards into one end of the tube (Figure 2).

4. Pull the wires through the tube and out the other end. Attach one end of each wire to a battery using sticky tape (Figure 3).

6. Cut out a small rectangle from some card. Cut it in two places (Figure 4).

7. Bend one edge away from you and the other edge towards you to make a propeller shape (Figures 4 and 5).

8. Using a pencil, make a small hole in the middle of the propeller and push it onto the spindle of your motor.

9. Reattach the end of the wire to the battery. Tape the battery inside the tube and watch what happens to the propeller (Figure 6).

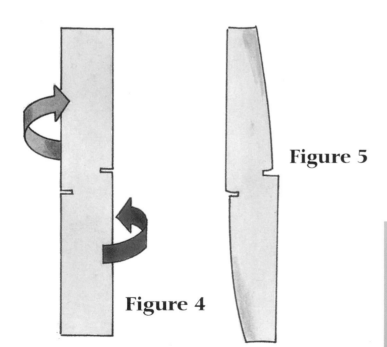

Figure 5

Figure 4

5. Take one wire off the battery to stop the motor working until you need it.

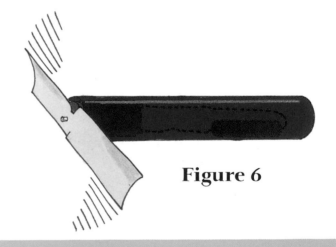

Figure 6

WHY IT WORKS

Electricity travels from the battery, through the wire, to the motor and back to the battery. This is an electrical circuit. The electricity makes the motor spindle spin. By adding a propeller, we can use electricity to spin it round and create wind.

What is electricity?

MAKE A TAPPER SWITCH

1. Bend a long strip of copper into the shape shown (Figure 1) and glue it onto a piece of wood.

2. Glue a small piece of copper onto the edge of the wood, so that it hangs over the edge.

3. Glue a piece of cork to the top end of the long piece of copper (Figure 1).

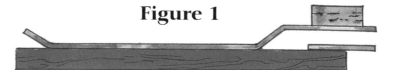

Figure 1

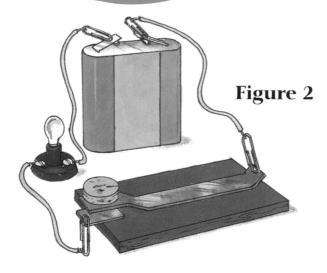

Figure 2

5. Connect the other end of the wire to one side of a battery (Figure 2).

6. Attach a paperclip to the small piece of copper. Then attach a wire to the paperclip and to a small bulb. Attach a wire from the bulb to the battery (Figure 2).

7. Press the cork to touch the small piece of copper and watch the bulb light up.

4. Attach a paperclip to the long piece of copper at the end furthest from the cork, and attach a piece of wire to the paperclip.

Unbelievable speed!
When you turn on a switch, the electric signal travels at 300,000 km/second
This is as fast as the speed of light.

MAKE A SIMPLE SWITCH

Make this simple circuit (see right) by firstly pushing a drawing pin into some wood with a paperclip under it. Connect the pin to a bulb and the bulb to a battery, using insulated wire. Connect the battery to a second drawing pin. Move the loose end of the clip towards the pin and see the bulb light up.

MAKE A DIMMER SWITCH

Soak a pencil in water and then split it in half down the middle (Figure 1). Glue it onto a piece of wood and attach a wire to each end of the pencil with crocodile clips. Connect one of the wires to a battery.

Connect the second wire to a light bulb. Attach another wire to the battery and to the other side of the bulb. Gradually slide one clip towards the other and watch the bulb get brighter (Figure 2).

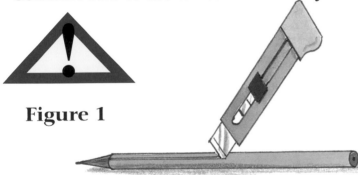

Figure 1

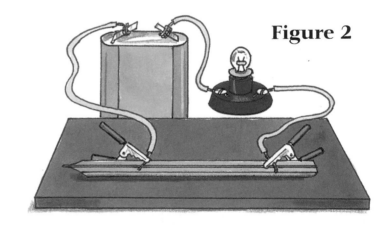

Figure 2

WHY IT WORKS

The graphite in the pencil is partially resistant to electricity, so the electricity finds it hard to go through. Therefore, when you move the clips apart the light gets dimmer as the electricity has to travel through more of the graphite.

Electricity travelling round a circuit can be stopped and started by a switch. Every day we use hundreds of switches and circuits to help us work, travel and prepare food.

Current

Electrical charge moving through a material is a current of electricity. For a current to flow there must be a circuit, or unbroken loop, for it to travel round. There must also be a force to push the charge along from something like a battery. Current is a measure of the amount of electrical charge transferred from one place to another in one second.

 ## See how current can make a motor spin

 METHOD NOTES
Make sure your paperclips are long enough to hold the coil above the magnets.

Materials
- a plastic cup
- 5 circular magnets
- 2 large paperclips
- insulated copper wire
- 4.5v battery
- a marker pen

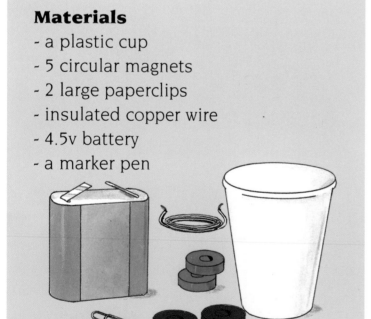

1. Wind the copper wire into a coil about 2.5 cm in diameter.

2. Wrap a short piece of wire once round the coil and leave 2 cm sticking out at each side.

3. Strip off the ends of the copper wire and blacken the top half of one of the stripped wires using a marker pen (Figure 1).

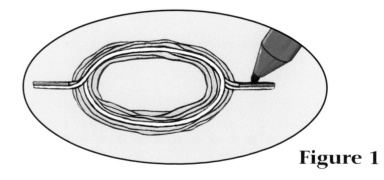

Figure 1

4. Turn the cup upside down and place two magnets on top. Carefully place three more magnets inside the cup underneath the other magnets so they hold each other in place (Figure 2).

5. Unfold two paperclips and tape them to the sides of the cup (Figure 2).

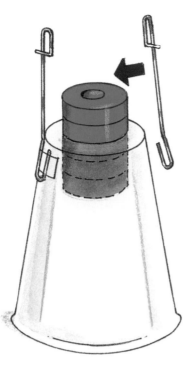

Figure 2

WHY IT WORKS

Electric current flowing through the wire coil causes one side of the coil to become a north pole and the other a south pole (see pages 30 to 33). The magnets on top of the cup repel and attract (or push and pull) the coil so that it spins round. Marking the wire black ensures that the current keeps the coil turning.

6. Place the coil in between the paperclips and balance it above the magnets. Use the two wires sticking out (Figure 3) to keep it in place.

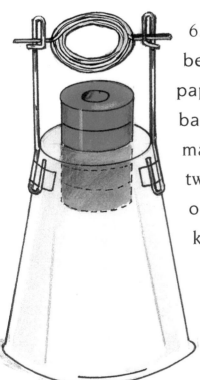

Figure 3

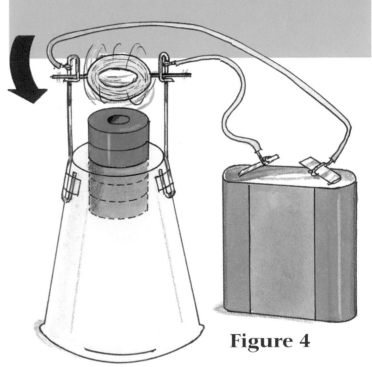

Figure 4

7. Attach two pieces of wire to the paperclips and then to a battery (Figure 4).

8. Give the coil a spin with your finger and watch what happens to your motor.

Current

Most objects allow electricity to flow through them, but not everything does it well. How well something allows electricity to flow is measured by its resistance.

CONDUCTORS AND INSULATORS

Attach two wires to each end of a battery using sticky tape. Attach the other end of one wire to a bulb and the end of the other to a crocodile clip. Attach a third wire from the bulb to another crocodile clip (Figure 1). You have made a simple circuit with a gap in it so that you can add in different objects and test them.

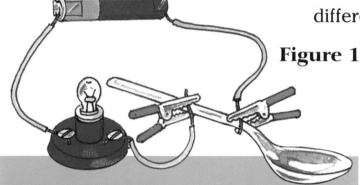

Figure 1

Now attach the two crocodile clips to different objects (Figure 2). Some household objects are conductors and some are insulators. Check the light bulb each time to see if electricity is flowing through the circuit.

Figure 2

WHY IT WORKS

If the object is a good conductor, the light bulb will shine. A poor conductor (a resistor) will make the bulb shine dimly and an insulator not at all.

Ouch that hurts!
Did you know that the bite of a South American Bushmaster snake can be treated by a series of electric shocks?

ELECTROPLATE A SPOON

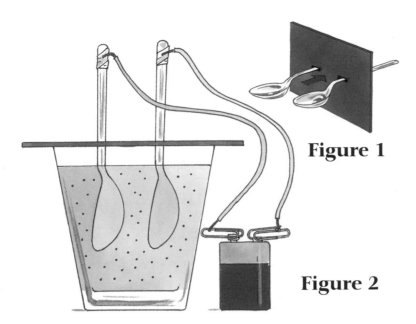

Figure 1

Figure 2

Push two metal spoons through a piece of card (Figure 1). Rest the card across a bowl containing copper sulphate solution. Attach a wire to the end of each spoon using sticky tape. Attach the other ends of the wires to a battery using paperclips (Figure 2). Watch what happens to the colour of the spoons. Then wash your hands thoroughly.

WHY IT WORKS

The electric current causes the copper in the solution to be attracted to the spoon connected to the negative battery terminal. The spoon becomes coated with copper. This works because the copper in the solution becomes positively charged.

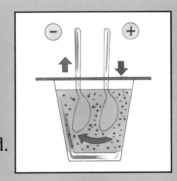

MAKE A BATTERY TESTER

Wrap 2 m of wire around a compass. Make sure you can still see north and south. Attach the two loose ends to a battery.

The greater the current travelling through the wire, the more the compass needle will move. Why not use this to test how much charge is in your batteries?

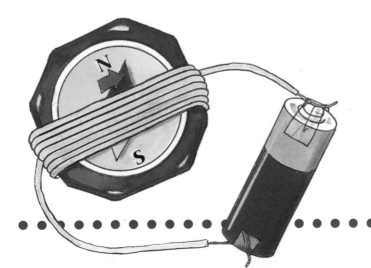

Current is the way electricity moves from one place to another. Different materials allow different amounts of electricity to go through them.

Batteries

Batteries are the most simple and convenient way of producing electricity. They contain stored chemical energy. The chemicals react with each other and produce an electrical charge. When the battery is connected in a circuit, this charge travels round the circuit as electrical current. Batteries come in all sizes – small ones in watches and large batteries to power cars.

Discover how a chemical reaction makes electricity

METHOD NOTES
Make sure you build your battery 'cells' in the right order – coin, paper towel then foil.

Materials
- lemon juice or salt
- 12 copper coins
- aluminium foil
- water
- scissors
- insulated wire
- paper towel
- a compass
- a glass
- a nail
- sticky tape

1. Draw round a coin and cut out 12 circles of foil (Figure 1).

2. Do the same with some paper towel.

3. Dissolve 10 teaspoons of salt in a glass of water (Figure 2) or add the juice of a lemon.

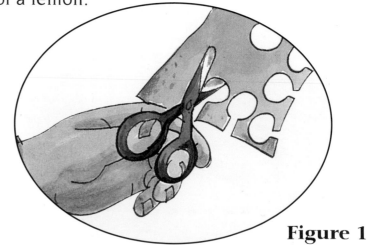

Figure 1

4. With your fingers carefully dampen the paper towel circles with the solution.

5. Make a tower by stacking the coins, paper towel and foil on top of each other.

Figure 2

WHY IT WORKS

The coins react with the foil and the salt or lemon solution to produce electricity. When you attach the wires, the current is conducted from one metal coin to another through the salt water and foil. This current attracts the compass needle. Try removing the nail and bringing the ends of the wires together in a darkened room. You may see a little spark.

Figure 3

Figure 4

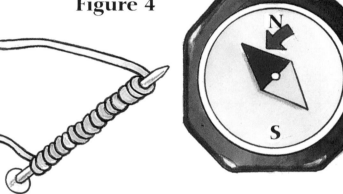

6. Wrap a wire tightly around a nail and attach the loose ends to the top and bottom of the pile with sticky tape (Figure 3).

7. Move the nail close to a compass and see how the needle moves (Figure 4). Make sure you wash your hands carefully.

How long?
Did you know that there is a battery that has been working since the year 1840!

Batteries

MAKE A CHARGE CARRIER

Ask an adult to help you push a nail through the lid of a film canister. Wrap some foil around the bottom two-thirds of the canister and then fill it almost full with water. Put the lid on and make sure the nail is pushed down into the water (Figure 1). Rub a polystyrene tray with some wool (Figure 2). Place an aluminium pie tin on top of it and touch the pie tin with your finger. There will be a spark.

Figure 1

Figure 2

Holding the canister by the foil, let the nail contact the pie tin (Figure 3). Don't touch the pie tin yourself. Now, touch the nail with your finger.

Figure 3

WHY IT WORKS

Rubbing the polystyrene tray makes the tray negatively charged. The pie tin sitting on the tray becomes negatively charged. The negative electrons jump onto you when you touch the tin. This leaves the tin positively charged and you negatively charged. Then, electrons move from the nail onto the positive pie tin. The nail is now positive. Finally, when you touch the nail, electrons are attracted from you into the nail. They are stored in the nail and in the water.

THE AMAZING DISAPPEARING INK
Show how a battery can create a chemical reaction

Don't breathe in the gas produced in this experiment.
Dissolve as much salt as you can in half a glass of water. Add some ink to the water and pour it into a saucer. Attach two wires to a battery and dip the other ends into the water. Can you see the colour of the ink disappear?

WHY IT WORKS
A chemical reaction produces bubbles of chlorine gas. This bleaches the ink and makes it disappear.

MAKE A WET BATTERY

Place a strip of zinc and a piece of copper pipe into a glass filled with white vinegar. Stick a piece of wire to each piece of metal.

Attach the other end of each wire to either side of a light emitting diode (LED). The LED should glow red. If not, swap the wires on the LED. You could try using two pieces of zinc and copper. Metal plates in a liquid can cause a chemical reaction, which creates electricity to power your LED.

Some batteries, called primary batteries, must be thrown away once their chemicals have been used up. Others, such as car batteries, can be recharged and used again. They are called secondary batteries.

Static electricity

Some materials don't let electricity pass through them but a static (still) electrical charge can be produced on their surface when they rub against certain other materials. This electrical charge can move when it is attracted by another charged object. When you take off your sweater, you might hear a crackling sound as you produce static electricity.

See how lightning can be made

METHOD NOTES
Do the last part of this experiment in a darkened room.

Materials
- a polystyrene tray
- an aluminium tray
- sticky tape
- scissors

1. Cut the corner off a polystyrene tray and stick it to the middle of an aluminium tray with sticky tape, to make a handle (Figure 1).

Figure 1

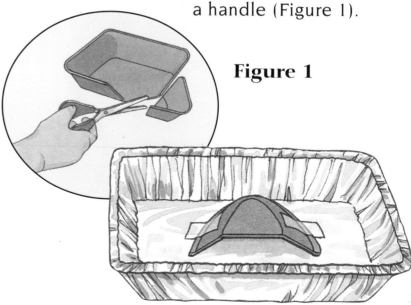

Figure 2

2. Rub the bottom of the polystyrene tray on your hair really fast. Rub it from side to side (Figure 2).

3. Place the polystyrene tray upside down on a table.

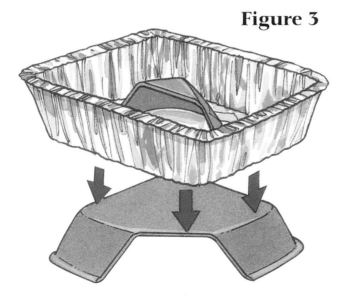

Figure 3

4. Pick up the aluminium tray by the handle and carefully drop it onto the polystyrene tray (Figure 3). Don't touch the polystyrene tray!

5. While the aluminium tray is still on the polystyrene tray, touch the aluminium tray with your finger. Watch what happens.

6. Pick up the aluminium tray by the handle and touch it again with your finger (Figure 4). Can you see the lightning each time you touch the aluminium tray?

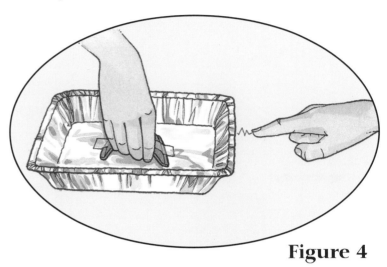

Figure 4

WHY IT WORKS

You create a negative charge on the polystyrene tray when you rub it on your hair. As you touch the aluminium tray, negative electrons leap to your hand. The second time, electrons jump from your hand to the positive tray and you see another spark.

19

Static electricity

MAKE AN ELECTROSCOPE

Cut two 1 cm by 4 cm strips of aluminium foil (Figure 1). Open out a paperclip and push it through the centre of a piece of card. Hang the two pieces of foil on the hook of the paperclip (Figure 2). Place the card over the top of a see-through glass so that the foil and paperclip hang inside (Figure 3).

Figure 1

Figure 2

Figure 3

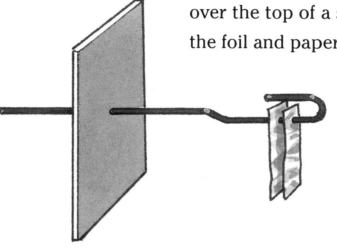

WHY IT WORKS

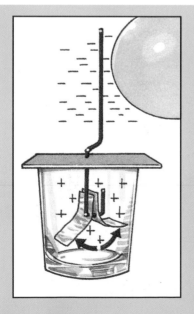

Bringing a charged object near to the paperclip moves electrons out of the foil. Each foil strip then has the same charge so they repel each other and push apart.

Bring different charged objects, like combs or balloons that you have been rubbing on your hair, close to the paperclip. Watch what happens to the foil.

THE AMAZING BENDING WATER
Show how electrical charge attracts water

Comb your hair a few times with a plastic comb. Turn on the tap and bring the comb close to the running water. Watch what happens to the flow of water.

WHY IT WORKS
The charged water coming from the tap is attracted to the charged comb and moves towards it, making it bend!

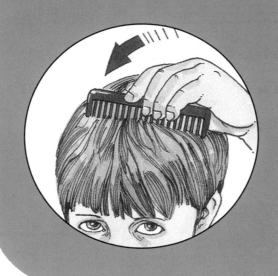

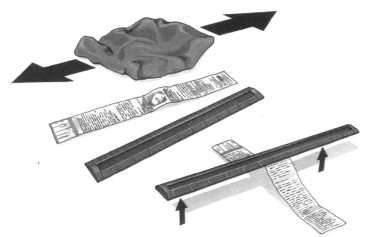

STATIC ELECTRICITY NEWSPAPER

Cut a strip of newspaper 30 cm by 5 cm. Put it on a table and stroke it 30 times with a woollen cloth. You can attract the newspaper using a plastic ruler.

Static electricity can be very powerful. The best example of this is lightning. Lightning contains a huge amount of electrical energy which is changed into light, heat and sound (thunder). The sparks caused by everyday static electricity are just small lightning bolts.

All around you

Have a look around you and count how many things you use every day that depend on electricity. Electricity is one of the easiest ways of producing light and heat in our world. Most electricity is produced by burning fossil fuels. Fossil fuels will not last forever so scientists are finding ways of producing electricity using wind, solar and water power. These sources are renewable.

Use electricity to make a secret room alarm

METHOD NOTES
When you have finished, hide your alarm under a rug or carpet so no one can see it.

Materials
- 4.5v battery
- a light bulb
- insulated wire
- stiff card
- aluminium foil
- sticky tape

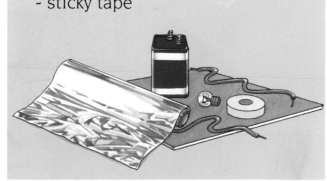

1. Fold a piece of card in half.
2. Wrap a strip of foil round each side of the card (Figure 1). Stick them in place with sticky tape.

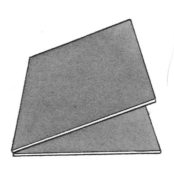

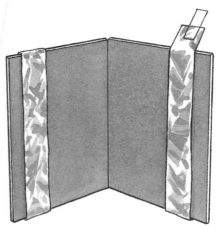

Figure 1

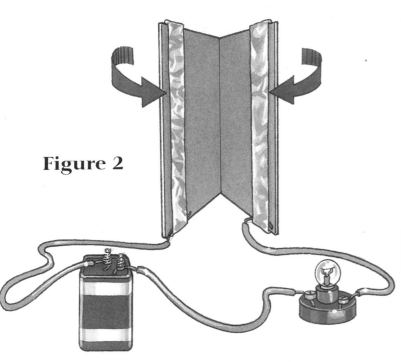

Figure 2

6. Place the card under a rug and hide the bulb so that only you can see it (Figure 3).

7. Watch what happens when the card closes and the foil strips touch each other.

Figure 3

3. Stick a piece of wire to the foil on each side using sticky tape.

4. Connect the other end of one of the wires to a battery.

5. Attach the other wire to a bulb and then attach a third wire from the bulb to the battery (Figure 2).

WHY IT WORKS

When your intruder steps on the card the foil strips touch each other. This completes the electrical circuit, which allows the electrical current to flow and light the bulb.

So much electricity!
If everyone only boiled the water they needed, instead of filling the kettle, we could save enough energy to light almost every street light in the UK!

Electricity heats metal objects to make them glow – this is how a light bulb produces light. You should always be careful not to touch metal that is connected in a circuit.

All around you

MAKE A HEAD TORCH

1. Cut a strip of card long enough to fit round your head. Staple the two ends together (Figure 1).

2. Attach one small battery to the side of the headband with sticky tape.

3. Cut a circle from card and carefully make a hole in the centre.

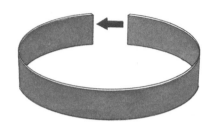

Figure 1

4. Attach two long pieces of insulated wire to the back of a bulb (Figure 2).

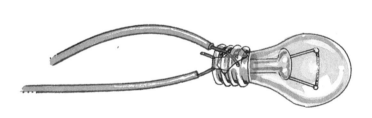

Figure 2

5. Push the bulb and wires backwards through the hole in the card circle (Figure 3).

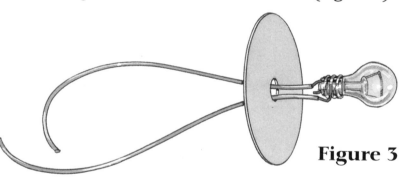

Figure 3

6. Stick the circle to the front of the headband.

7. Attach each wire to the battery at the side and stick the wires in place around the headband.

8. Your circuit is connected and the bulb should now glow (Figure 4).

9. Place the head torch on your head and try it out. Why not try it tonight to read in bed?

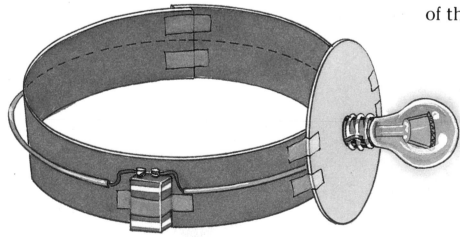

Figure 4

THE AMAZING ELECTRICAL BALLOON
See a balloon light a fluorescent bulb

Ask an adult to help you with this experiment. In a dark room, rub a balloon from side to side on your hair. Do this lots of times. Touch the balloon to the end of a fluorescent light bulb and watch what happens.

WHY IT WORKS
You should see small sparks and the bulb should glow. Electrons move from the balloon to the bulb causing small sparks inside the bulb.

Figure 1

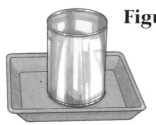

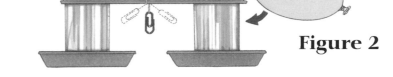

Figure 2

STATIC ELECTRICITY BELL

Place two empty metal food cans on plastic trays (Figure 1). Tie a metal paperclip to some cotton and tie the cotton round another plastic tray. Rest this across the cans. Rub a balloon on your hair. Hold it next to one of the cans (Figure 2).

Static electricity causes the paperclip to be attracted and repelled. It swings between the cans, hitting them like a bell.

In the future, fossil fuels will run out. This is why new sources for electricity are always being sought.

What is magnetism?

Magnetism is a force that causes attraction or repulsion between objects. Magnets always contain metal. The atoms in a magnetic material, like iron or steel, all point in the same direction. Magnetism is used in many everyday things, such as telephones and motors. It is even used to help ships find their way in stormy seas.

Make a magnetic boat to see how magnets work

METHOD NOTES
Make sure you use waterproof glue for this experiment.

Materials
- a bowl of water
- card
- a skewer
- a cork
- a small magnet
- a paperclip
- waterproof glue
- a large strong magnet
- 2 dowelling rods
- scissors
- sticky tape

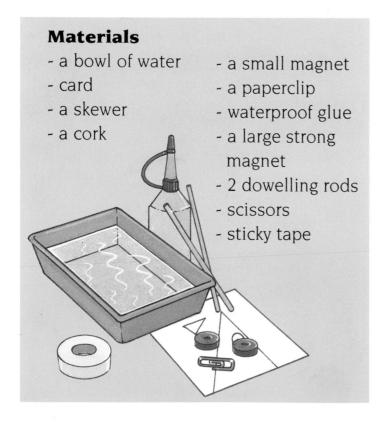

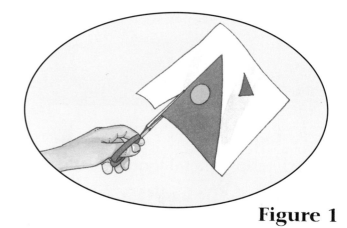

Figure 1

1. Cut some sail and flag shapes out of card and decorate them (Figure 1).
2. Stick the sails onto a dowelling rod to make a mast for your boat.

Figure 2

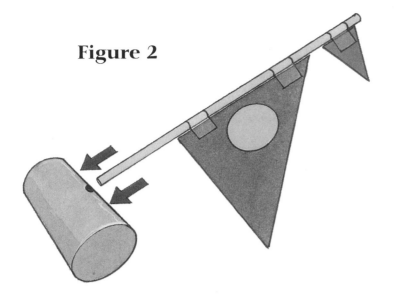

5. Unbend a paperclip as shown and glue a small magnet to the bottom of it (Figure 4).

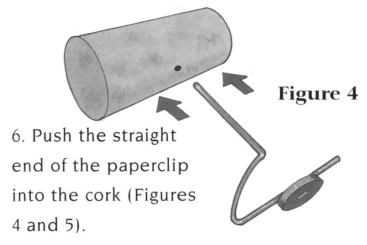

Figure 4

6. Push the straight end of the paperclip into the cork (Figures 4 and 5).

3. Make a small hole in the side of a cork with a skewer and push your mast into it (Figure 2).

7. Float your boat in a bowl of water.

8. Use your magnet on the dowelling rod to move your boat from underneath the bowl (Figure 5).

4. Glue a large strong magnet onto the end of the other dowelling rod (Figure 3).

Figure 3

WHY IT WORKS

You can control the boat from underneath because the magnetic force travels through water. The two magnets attract or repel each other, depending which way up they are, causing your boat to move.

Figure 5

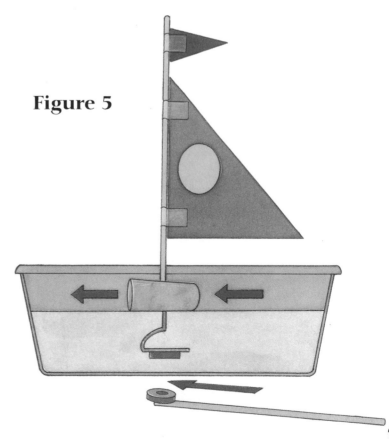

When the atoms of an object all point in different directions, the object is not magnetic. Some things, like plastic, wood and some metals, can never be picked up with a magnet.

What is magnetism?

EXPERIMENT WITH MAGNETS

You can test the strength of a magnet by seeing how many paperclips or nails it can pick up. A strong magnet will pick up lots. Why not try experimenting with some household objects to see what else your magnet can pick up.

Try metal objects like keys, cutlery and coins and other objects made from wood, plastic or rubber. Which ones can you pick up?

THE AMAZING DISAPPEARING SONG
See the effect of magnetism on recorded sound

Take an old, unwanted cassette and wind it back to the start. Unravel part of the tape.

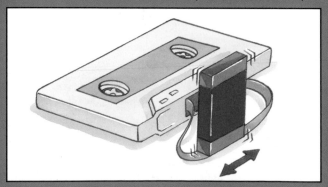

Wipe a magnet over it backwards and forwards several times. Wind the cassette back to the beginning and play it to see if the sound has changed.

WHY IT WORKS
The tape in cassettes is plastic tape with a coating of magnetic particles arranged in a regular pattern. When you rub the magnet over the tape, you rearrange the particles and distort the recorded sound.

MAGNETISE AND DEMAGNETISE A NAIL

Take a large steel nail and bring a compass near it. Does the compass needle move? Point one end of the nail to north and place it on a piece of wood, or outside on some tarmac. Put on a pair of safety goggles and hit the nail 50 times with a hammer (Figure 1).

Figure 1

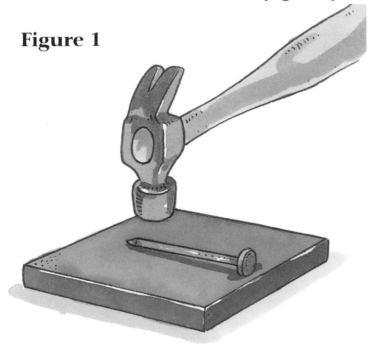

Again, see what effect it has on a compass (Figure 2). Turn the nail round so it points south and hit it 50 more times. How does the needle move this time? Now line up the nail in an east–west direction and hit it 50 times more. Does the compass needle stay still this time?

WHY IT WORKS

When the nail is lined up with the north and south poles of the Earth and then hammered, it becomes magnetised. Hammering a nail like this makes the atoms point in the same direction. Hammering the nail when it is pointing east–west makes the atoms line up across the nail and it appears demagnetised.

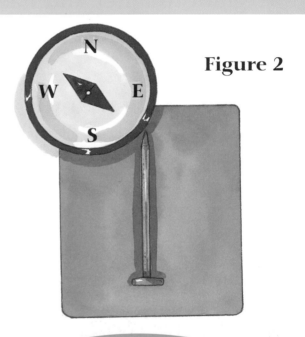

Figure 2

Magnetism is an invisible force, but we use its power anywhere we can. It is used for generating electricity, for scientific research and it is used in all electrical motors.

Magnetic poles

Every magnet has two poles – north and south. If you broke a magnet into tiny pieces, each piece would still have a north and a south pole. The south pole of one magnet seeks the north pole of another magnet and repels the other's south pole. The Earth behaves like a giant magnet and has a magnetic north and south pole, which are close to the geographic North and South Poles.

See how magnets can show you the way

METHOD NOTES
Draw the compass points on the card very carefully.

Materials
- a cup
- a needle
- a cork
- a protractor
- water
- a magnet
- card
- sticky tape
- scissors

1. Cut out a circle of card and then cut a hole in the centre slightly smaller than the diameter of your cup (Figure 1).

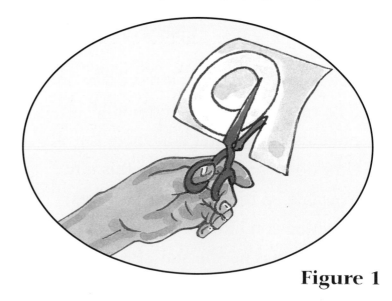

Figure 1

2. Fill the cup with water almost to the top (Figure 2).

3. Make the needle magnetic by stroking it with one end of a magnet (Figure 3). Do this 30 times in the same direction.

4. Carefully cut a cork lengthways and stick the needle onto it (Figure 4).

5. Float the cork in the water with the needle facing upwards.

6. Using a protractor, divide the circle into four equal parts and draw on the four compass points – north, south, east and west (Figure 5).

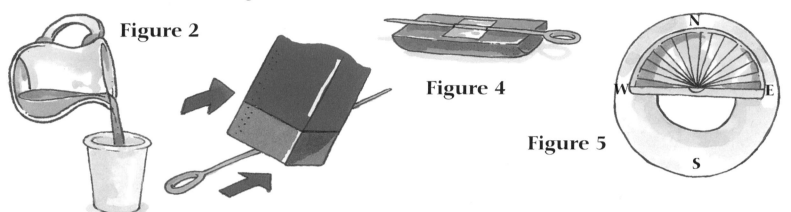

Figure 2

Figure 3

Figure 4

Figure 5

7. Place the card circle on top of the cup so that the needle is pointing north to south (Figure 6).

8. Take your compass outside and try it out.

WHY IT WORKS

Stroking a needle magnetises it by lining up all the atoms in the same direction. The north-seeking pole of every magnet always points to the magnetic north pole of the Earth. The north-seeking pole of a magnet is really its south pole as it is attracted to the magnetic north pole of Earth. As magnetic north is close to the geographic North Pole, this means you can always find out which way is north, south, east and west.

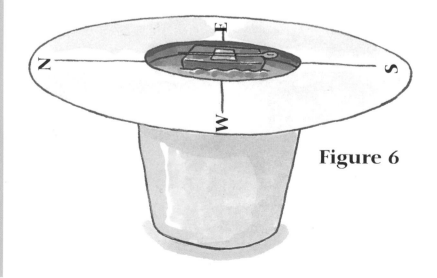

Figure 6

Magnetic poles

There are two types of magnet – permanent and temporary. They both have a north and south pole. It is the pushing and pulling forces of magnets that make them so useful.

MAKE A COMPASS IN A GLASS

Place a needle on a table and stroke it in the same direction with one end of a magnet about 30 times (Figure 1). Fold a strip of card in half and stick the magnetised needle to the inside. Fold the card over the top of the needle (Figure 2). This is your compass strip.

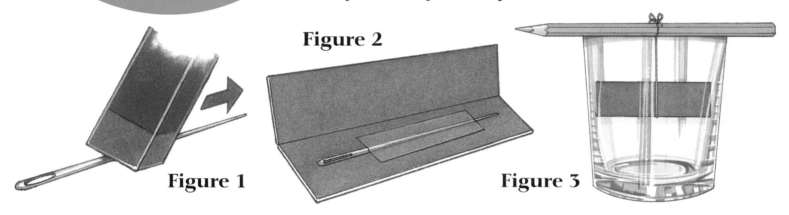

Figure 2

Figure 1

Figure 3

Tie one end of a piece of string round the middle of the card and tie the other end around the middle of a pencil. Place the pencil across the top of a glass.

The compass strip should hang inside the glass (Figure 3). Take your compass outside and watch the needle always point in the north–south direction.

Floating trains

Maglev trains don't have wheels. Instead, they float above the track because of magnetic repulsion between the tracks and the train. They can travel up to 480 km/h!

THE AMAZING FLOATING MAGNETS
Show the effect of magnetic levitation

Stick some modelling clay to a table. Push a piece of dowelling into the clay. Make sure the dowelling is just smaller in diameter than the centre of the magnets. Put four or five doughnut magnets over the dowelling. All the magnets must have their north poles facing other north poles.

WHY IT WORKS

When the magnets are placed north–north or south–south, they will 'float' above each other. This is because similar poles repel each other.

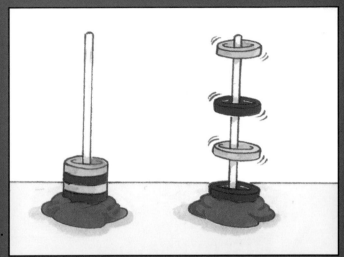

INSECT WINDOW CLEANERS

Cut out some insect shapes from card and decorate them. Glue a small magnet to the back of each one.

Glue a small piece of felt on top of the magnet. Place your insect onto a window pane and hold it in place with another magnet on the other side. Move your insect around to clean the window. Only do this if you are on the ground floor.

Opposite magnetic poles attract and similar poles repel. The south pole of a magnet is attracted to the north pole of the Earth. Compass needles work like this to help us find our way.

Magnetic fields

The area around a magnet is called the magnetic field. Magnetic fields are invisible, but we know that the field lines join the north end of a magnet to the south. A magnetic field is created by the magnetism of a permanent magnet or by an electric current. The larger the magnet, and the closer an object is to the magnet, the greater the force of the magnetic field.

Discover what magnetic fields look like

METHOD NOTES
Make sure that you take the label off the baby oil bottle before you start.

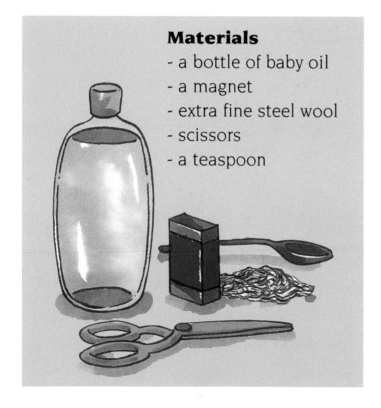

Materials
- a bottle of baby oil
- a magnet
- extra fine steel wool
- scissors
- a teaspoon

1. Carefully open a bottle of baby oil.
2. Unroll the extra fine steel wool and cut across it to get very short fibres. Cut enough to fill a teaspoon (Figure 1), but no more or the experiment won't work.

Figure 1

3. Bunch the fibres together and drop them into the bottle (Figure 2).

4. Put the top on and shake the bottle by rotating it round and round. Don't shake it up and down.

Figure 2

5. Hold a strong magnet a few centimetres from the side of the bottle and watch what happens (Figure 3).

Figure 3

6. Don't hold it too close or all the fibres will clump together.

7. Try different ends of the magnet or more than one magnet to see what difference it makes to the pattern. Rotate the bottle after each go.

Why not try this experiment with some short pieces of black hair cut from an old doll or party wig. Bring charged objects, like a balloon rubbed on your hair, towards the side of the bottle and see the patterns.

WHY IT WORKS

Iron filings align in strong magnetic fields so that all the north poles of the iron atoms point in the same direction. This reveals the shape of the three-dimensional magnetic field patterns. Small fibres of hair behave in a similar way when exposed to electric fields.

Charged balloons create electric fields by static electricity. The fibres begin to settle after 15 seconds so you need to keep rotating the bottle if you want to keep experimenting.

Magnetic fields

Invisible magnetic force fields are able to pass through some liquids and everyday objects made of glass and wood.

MAKE A MAGNETIC SHIELD

Glue two dowelling rods along each side of a piece of card. Glue another card on the dowelling so there is a thin gap between the two cards. Glue a strong magnet to the top edge of the card. Holding your shield by the end without the magnet, hover it above some paperclips. Does it pick them up?

WHY IT WORKS

When you insert the lolly stick, the paperclips stay hanging, but when you insert the knife they fall off. The magnetic field lines from the magnet pass through the lolly stick, but the metal knife acts as a shield and stops the field lines from passing through.

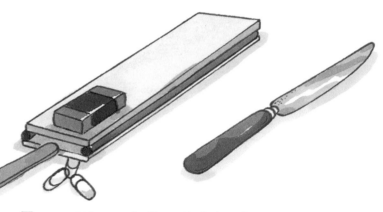

Try putting a lolly stick in the gap. Does it still attract the clips? Place a metal knife in between and watch what happens to the paperclips now.

Stormy weather

Did you know that the Earth experiences magnetic storms that can last for days at a time? The storms happen when electrically charged particles from the Sun get trapped in the magnetic field of the Earth.

THE AMAZING JUMPING SNAKE
Show how electric current can create a magnetic field

Cut a strip of foil 40 cm by 1 cm and place it on a table. Put a horseshoe magnet across the strip. Attach two wires to a battery and stick one end of one wire to one end of the strip. Quickly touch the other wire to the other end of the foil and watch the foil snake jump. Don't leave the battery connected for long and don't touch the foil – it could be hot.

WHY IT WORKS
An electric current flows through the foil and this creates a magnetic field. This reacts with the magnetic field of the horseshoe magnet and causes the foil to be attracted and 'jump' towards it.

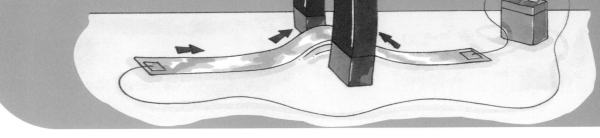

MAKE A SWINGING MAGNET

Build a stand using three pieces of dowelling. Push it into some modelling clay and place some round magnets underneath it. They must all have the same pole facing up. Tie a magnet onto some string and hang it from the stand. Swing it over the magnets and see how it reacts to the magnetic fields.

The magnetic fields of two or more magnets can react with each other to cause movement. Although magnetic fields are invisible, the movements they cause are fascinating to watch and experiment with.

Electromagnetism

An electromagnet is formed when a copper wire, connected to a battery, is coiled round a metal object like a nail. The electricity from the battery flows into the coil and produces a temporary magnetic field. Electromagnets come in all shapes and sizes. You use them in everyday items, such as doorbells and switches.

See how electricity magnetises metal

METHOD NOTES
Make sure the ruler you use has a hole in the end of it.

Materials
- a horseshoe bolt
- insulated copper wire
- a long elastic band
- a long ruler
- a cotton reel
- a jar or glass
- a battery
- 2 dowelling rods
- sticky tape
- string
- modelling clay

1. Wrap some wire tightly round a horseshoe bolt leaving two long ends free (Figure 1).

Figure 1

2. Feed the two pieces of wire through the hole in the end of a ruler and tape them down the length of the ruler (Figure 2).

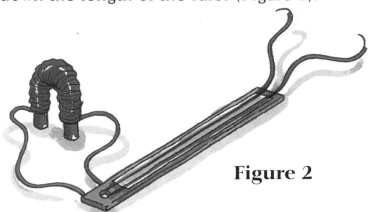

Figure 2

3. Attach the two wires to a battery.

4. Secure the ruler to the side of a glass or jar with an elastic band (Figure 3).

5. Lie the glass on its side and secure it in place with some modelling clay.

6. Tie a piece of string to the middle of the horseshoe bolt and feed it through the hole in the ruler so the bolt is dangling from the ruler (Figure 3).

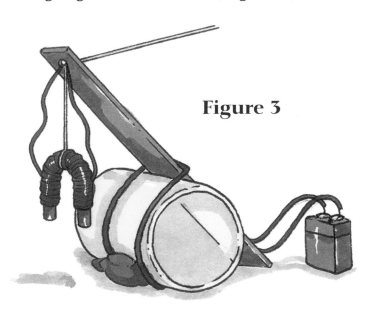

Figure 3

7. Tape a piece of dowelling to the ruler and push a cotton reel on to one end (Figure 4).

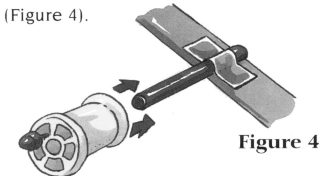

Figure 4

8. Put a piece of dowelling in the cotton reel to act as a handle (Figure 4).

9. Tape the string to the cotton reel and wrap the rest of the string around it.

10. Wind the magnet up and down to pick up objects (Figure 5).

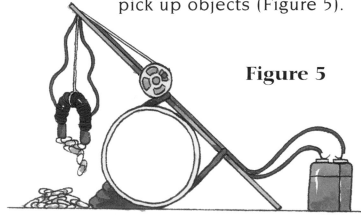

Figure 5

WHY IT WORKS

The battery in your circuit sends an electric current into the wire around the metal bolt. This creates a magnetic field and turns the bolt into an electromagnet, or temporary magnet. Certain objects will be attracted to it so you can pick them up.

Electromagnetism

MAKE A RAILWAY SIGNAL

1. Wrap 2 m of wire round a straw leaving 10 cm free at each end. Put a nail half inside the straw (Figure 1).
2. Push a drawing pin through one end of another straw, about 2 cm from the top, and into a piece of thick card. Make sure the straw hangs loosely.
3. Cut out a signal arm shape from some card and make a small hole in the top of it (Figure 2).

Figure 1

WHY IT WORKS

When the battery is connected, the electric current flows through the wire coil and creates a magnetic field. The magnetised coil of wire attracts the nail inside the straw and pulls it to the left. This pulls the straw on the card and moves the signal arm down.

4. Pin it to the card near the top of the straw using a drawing pin.
5. Wrap one end of a paperclip round the top of the straw and hook the other end through the signal arm (Figure 2).

Figure 2

6. Place the straw with the nail in it on the table so that the head of the nail is hooked behind the straw (Figure 3).
7. Tape the wires to a battery and watch what happens to the signal arm (Figure 4).

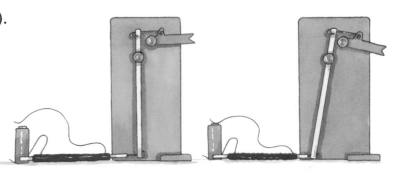

Figure 3   **Figure 4**

Turn on a radio and tune it so it is in between stations. Turn it up so there is a loud hissing noise. Hold an electromagnet close to the radio and listen as the sound changes when you connect the wires to the battery.

WHY IT WORKS

The electromagnet sends out electric current signals that the radio receives as clicking noises.

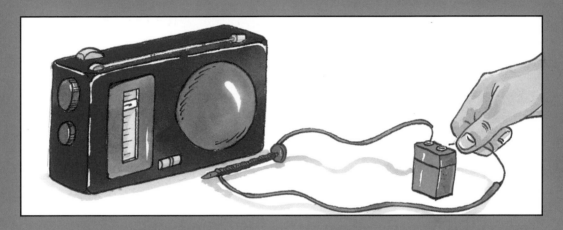

Figure 1

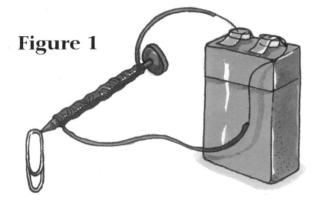

MAKE AN ELECTROMAGNET

Try experimenting with a simple electromagnet made from a nail, wire and battery (Figure 1) and see how powerful it is.

See how many paperclips you can pick up at once. How does it compare to a permanent magnet? Try adding extra batteries into your circuit or extra wire to your nail and see what happens.

The strength of an electromagnet depends on the number of turns in the coil and the amount of the current travelling through the wire.

 Amazing magnets

Magnets are incredibly versatile. They can be used as switches to turn machines on and off, as powerful cranes to lift heavy objects safely or as simple fridge magnets to stick your shopping list to the freezer. The magnets in telephones, televisions and radios even help change electrical impulses into sounds.

Make a coin sorter to see how magnets are used in everyday life

METHOD NOTES
Make sure you fold the card carefully to make the right shapes for the coin slots.

Materials

- a shoe box
- card
- a magnet
- coins
- iron and steel washers
- sticky tape
- scissors

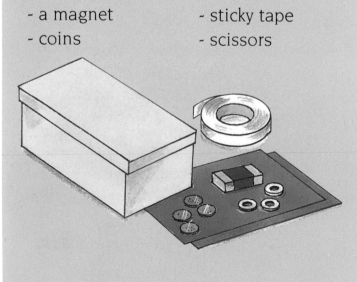

1. Cut a slot in one end of a shoe box. Make it about the length of a coin.

2. Cut out a strip of card and fold it into an 'L' shape (Figure 1).

3. Cut another strip of card and fold it 2 cm from the top. Tape a magnet to the top of the card (Figure 2).

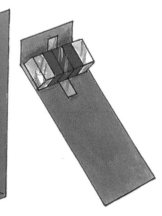

Figure 1

Figure 2

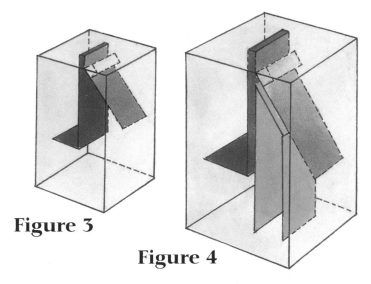

Figure 3

Figure 4

5. Tape the other card with the magnet at the top to the right of the slot (Figure 3).

6. Fold a third strip of card to fit in the triangular space between the other two pieces of card and tape it in place (Figure 4).

7. Drop your coins and washers down the slot and see which side they fall (Figure 5).

4. Tape the 'L'-shaped card inside the box to the left of the slot.

WHY IT WORKS

Some coins are made from non-magnetic metals. They are not attracted to the magnet and fall straight down. Iron and steel are magnetic metals and are attracted to the magnet. They fall down the right side of the box.

Figure 5

Magnetic creatures

Did you know that some birds, insects and fish have very small magnets in their bodies? Biologists know that these magnets help animals find their way when migrating.

Magnets are extremely good at finding metal hidden in other objects. In fact, a magnet could even find a needle in a haystack! You'd be surprised where metal can be found.

Amazing magnets

MAKE A SPINNING MAGNET

1. Mould some modelling clay and stick it onto a flat surface.

2. Carefully push the sharp end of a needle into some modelling clay (Figure 1).

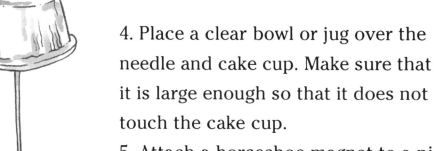

Figure 1

3. Place an aluminium cake cup onto the other end of the needle (Figure 2).

Figure 2

4. Place a clear bowl or jug over the needle and cake cup. Make sure that it is large enough so that it does not touch the cake cup.

5. Attach a horseshoe magnet to a piece of string and rotate it above the bowl (Figure 3). Watch what happens to the aluminium cake cup.

Figure 3

WHY IT WORKS

The magnetic field from the spinning magnet causes a very weak electric current in the aluminium cake cup. This current, along with the magnetic field, creates an electromagnetic field which turns the cake cup into a temporary magnet. The cake cup is then pulled around by the magnet hanging above it and it starts to spin.

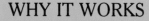

Place a handful of cereal in a see-through plastic bag. Drag a magnet across the outside of the bag. Look closely to see if the magnet has attracted anything to it.

WHY IT WORKS
Most cereals today contain added iron. When you place a magnet near the cereal, very small iron particles are attracted to the magnet. You could try the same experiment with sand as this also contains tiny iron particles.

MAGNETS AND ELECTRICITY IN NATURE
The Ancient Greeks and Chinese discovered that some rocks, minerals and meteorites are natural magnets.

These 'lodestones' can attract small pieces of iron and they always point in the same direction when they are held by a piece of string. Amber is a fossilized resin. It becomes electrically charged when it is rubbed and can attract small bits of straw.

Make a list of all the things you can find that use magnets. Think about whether they use a magnet or an electromagnet. Would they still work if the magnet wasn't there?

Glossary

Atoms

Tiny particles that make up a substance. Atoms in a magnetised material all point in the same direction.

Attraction

An electrical or magnetic force that pulls two or more objects together.

Conductor

A substance through which an electric current can flow. Metals are usually good conductors. Plastic and wood are usually poor conductors.

Electric charge

A substance has electric charge if it is positive or negative. If the substance gains electrons, it becomes more negative and if it loses electrons, it becomes more positive. Electric forces exist between charged particles.

Electrical circuit

The path that an electric current flows along. This must be an unbroken loop or the electricity will not flow.

Electrical current

A flow of electric charge, often around a circuit. Current flows from the negative terminal of a battery, around the circuit and to the positive battery terminal.

Electrical motor

A machine that turns electricity into movement using a magnet.

Electromagnet

An iron or steel object surrounded by a coil of wire that acts like a magnet when a current flows through the wire.

Electrons

In each atom there are one or more electrons. Each electron carries a negative electrical charge. The flow of electrons is what we call electricity.

Insulator

A substance that cannot conduct electric current at all. Rubber is an insulator.

Magnetic field

The space around a magnet where the magnet has magnetic influence. Magnetic objects in this field are pulled towards the magnet.

Magnetic poles

Areas on a magnet or on the Earth (north and south) where the force of attraction or repulsion is strongest.

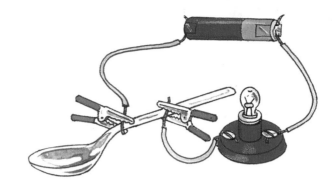

Repulsion

Electrical or magnetic forces that are given out by two or more objects. These forces push against each other to drive the objects apart.

Resistance

The ability of a substance to slow down the flow of electric current. Graphite is an example of a resistor.

Solution

This is a fluid where one substance has dissolved completely in another one.

Static electricity

Electricity that results from friction and does not flow as a current. It can jump from one material to another, as seen in lightning.

Index

amber 45
atoms 8, 26, 28, 29, 31, 35, 46
attraction 11, 18, 20, 25, 26, 27, 33, 36, 39, 40, 43, 45, 46, 47

batteries 6, 7, 8, 9, 10, 11, 12, 13, 14-17, 22, 23, 24, 37, 38, 39, 40, 44, 46
  primary 17
  secondary 17
  wet 17

chemical energy 14, 16
chemical reaction 14, 17
chlorine gas 17
compass 13, 14, 15, 29, 30, 31, 32, 33
conductor 12, 15, 46

demagnetise 29

Earth 29, 30, 31, 33, 36, 47
electrical charge 8, 10, 14, 16, 18, 19, 20, 21, 35, 36, 45, 46, 47
electrical circuit 7, 9, 10, 12, 14, 23, 24, 28, 41, 46
electrical current 10-13, 14, 15, 23, 34, 37, 39, 40, 41, 44, 46, 47
electrical impulses 6, 42
electrical motor 46
electric fields 35
electric shocks 12
electromagnet 38, 39, 40, 41, 46
electromagnetic field 44
electromagnetism 38-41, 45
electrons 8, 16, 19, 20, 25, 46
electroplating 13
electroscope 20

fossil fuels 22, 25, 42

geographic poles 30, 31
graphite 9, 47

heat 6, 21, 22, 24

insulators 12, 47

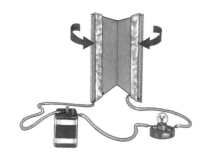

light 21, 22, 24
light bulbs 6, 8, 9, 12, 22, 23, 24, 25
light emitting diode (LED) 17
lightning 18, 21, 47
lodestones 45

Maglev trains 32
magnetic fields 34-37, 38, 39, 40, 44, 47
magnetic levitation 33
magnetic poles 11, 29, 30-33, 35, 37, 47
magnetic storms 36
magnetise 29, 31, 32, 38, 40, 46
magnet, permanent 32, 34, 41
magnet, temporary 32, 39, 44, 46
motor 6, 7, 10, 11, 26, 29

renewable energy 22
repulsion 11, 20, 25, 26, 27, 30, 32, 33, 47
resistance 9, 12, 47

solution 13, 15
static electricity 18-21, 25, 35, 47
switches 8, 9, 42
  dimmer 9
  simple 9
  tapper 8